OUR
GRE★T
STATES

WHAT'S GREAT ABOUT
TENNESSEE?

✸ Jenny Fretland VanVoorst

⌐ LERNER PUBLICATIONS COMPANY ✳ MINNEAPOLIS

CONTENTS

TENNESSEE WELCOMES YOU! ✳ 4

NASHVILLE ✳ 6

BELL WITCH CAVE ✳ 8

SMOKY MOUNTAINS ✳ 10

DOLLYWOOD ✳ 12

THE LOST SEA ADVENTURE ✳ 14

TENNESSEE AQUARIUM ✳ 16

Content Consultant: Bob Hutton, PhD,
Department of History, University of Tennessee

Lerner Publications Company
A division of Lerner Publishing Group, Inc.
241 First Avenue North
Minneapolis, MN 55401 USA

For reading levels and more information, look
up this title at www.lernerbooks.com.

Main body text set in ITC Franklin Gothic Std
Book Condensed 12/15.
Typeface provided by Adobe Systems.

Library of Congress Cataloging-in-Publication
Data

Fretland VanVoorst, Jenny, 1972-
    What's great about Tennessee? / by
Jenny Fretland VanVoorst.
        pages cm. — (Our great states)
    Includes index.
    ISBN 978-1-4677-3392-2 (library
binding : alkaline paper)
    ISBN 978-1-4677-4718-9 (eBook)
    1. Tennessee—Juvenile literature. I.
Title.
F436.3.F74 2015
976.8—dc23   2014003888

Manufactured in the United States of America
1 – PC – 7/15/14

LOOKOUT MOUNTAIN ✳ 18

SHILOH NATIONAL MILITARY PARK ✳ 20

MEMPHIS ✳ 22

THE PEABODY DUCK MARCH ✳ 24

TENNESSEE BY MAP ✳ 26
TENNESSEE FACTS ✳ 28
GLOSSARY ✳ 30
FURTHER INFORMATION ✳ 31
INDEX ✳ 32

TENNESSEE Welcomes You!

Welcome to Tennessee! If you're looking for great music and food, you're visiting the right place. Nashville and Memphis are two cities known for live music and delicious southern food. Listen to country or blues music, and try some tasty barbecue ribs. Or maybe you would prefer a trip to the Tennessee Aquarium. There are hundreds of sea animals to check out. Take an afternoon hike in the Smoky Mountains. Explore the trails near the Tennessee River. There is something for everyone! Tennessee has a lot to see, so let's get started. Read on to learn about ten things that make this a great state!

MISSOURI

KENTUCKY

VIRGINIA

Cumberland River

CUMBERLAND PLATEAU

Clinch River

Johnson City

Clarksville

Knoxville

NORTH CAROLINA

Nashville

Mississippi River

Tennessee River

Clingmans Dome
(6,643 feet/2,025 m)

S M O K Y   M O U N T A I N S

Pigeon River

Franklin

Murfreesboro

Great Smoky Mountains National Park

Duck River

Jackson

Miles
0 10 20 30 40
0   20   40   60
Kilometers

Chattanooga

Bartlett

Memphis

GEORGIA

MISSISSIPPI

ALABAMA

Explore Tennessee's cities and all the places in between! Just turn the page to find out about the VOLUNTEER STATE. >

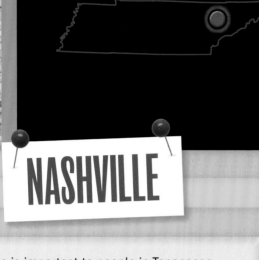

NASHVILLE

650 WSM

> Music is important to people in Tennessee. And nowhere is music bigger than in Nashville. The city is known as the country music capital of the world. Visit the Country Music Hall of Fame and Museum. Stop at the listening booths to hear different songs. Try out instruments at the Musical Petting Zoo. There are guitars and banjos to test. Be sure to stop in the Hall of Fame rotunda. Find your favorite singers' plaques on the walls.

Take in a show at the Grand Ole Opry. The Grand Ole Opry started as a radio show in 1925. Famous singers perform here. You may find a new favorite. Sign up for a backstage tour. You'll see photos of famous singers and maybe get to go onstage!

End your day at Nashville's Adventure Science Center. You can go through astronaut training in the Space Chase room. Find out what you would weigh on Jupiter! Or check out the Adventure Tower. You'll find new activities on all seven levels.

You can watch country music videos in the Country Music Hall of Fame and Museum.

Many of the restaurants in Nashville feature live music every night of the week.

7

BELL WITCH CAVE

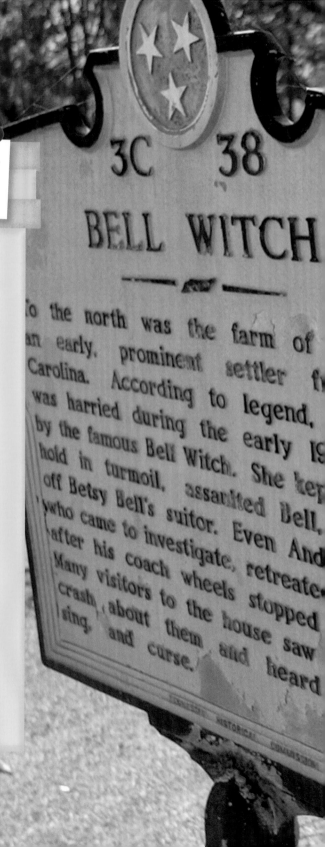

> If you're looking for something spooky, visit the Bell Witch Cave. It is home to one of the most famous hauntings in Tennessee. The Bell Witch story is even taught in Tennessee schools.

Stop in Adams for a tour of the cave and the cabin. You can explore the cave and hear stories of the Bell Witch. Locals say she lived in this cave. The witch haunted the Bell family back in the 1800s, but no one has seen her since. You can also walk through a replica of the Bell family's cabin. Listen for strange sounds like the ones the family heard. Look at photos, books, and documents from the family too. You may see Carney Bell dress up as his great-great-great-great grandfather John Bell in a play about the Bell family.

Visit around Halloween for an even scarier tour. You'll enjoy Bell Witch Fest. After your tour of the cave and the cabin, end the night with a haunted hayride.

In a book about the Bell Witch, illustrations portray the Bells' cabin and their daughter Betsy, who some say saw the ghost.

9

SMOKY MOUNTAINS

> Great Smoky Mountains National Park is the most visited national park in the United States. It has more than 800 miles (1,287 kilometers) of hiking trails. Many plants and animals live here. Put your hiking boots on and check it out!

Climb Clingmans Dome. It is the highest point in the state. Visit Cades Cove Riding Stables, and rent a horse for horseback riding. Or rent a bike. Try biking the 11-mile (18 km) Cades Cove Loop Road.

You can also pick a more adventurous activity. Enjoy whitewater rafting on the Pigeon River. Or ride a zip line through the forest.

CHEROKEE NATION

The Great Smoky Mountains are home to some of the Cherokee people. More Cherokee people once lived in other areas of Tennessee. But those who did not live in the Smokies were forced to move in 1838. The Indian Removal Act forced most of them off the land. They had to move west. Their path is known as the Trail of Tears. The Cherokee people living in the Smokies created the Eastern Band Nation.

You can look down over the Smokies at the top of Clingmans Dome.

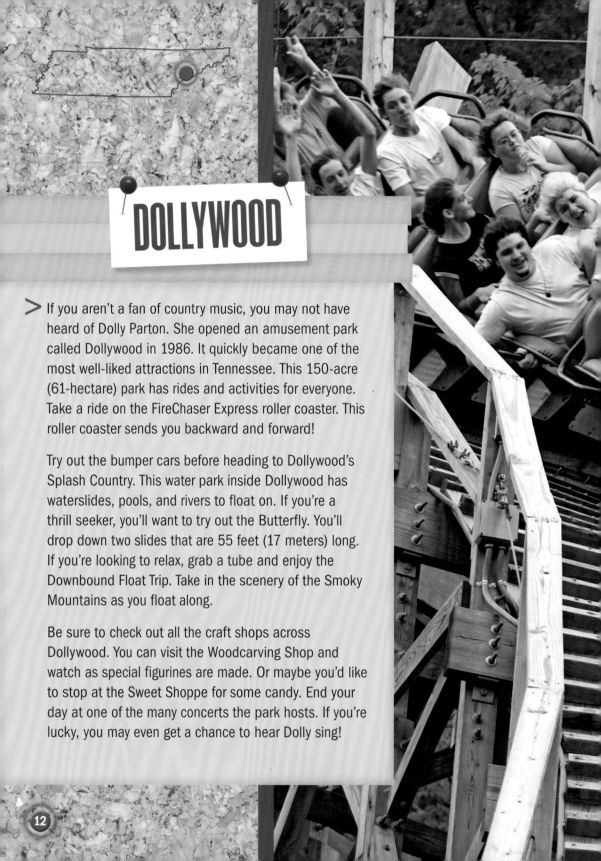

DOLLYWOOD

> If you aren't a fan of country music, you may not have heard of Dolly Parton. She opened an amusement park called Dollywood in 1986. It quickly became one of the most well-liked attractions in Tennessee. This 150-acre (61-hectare) park has rides and activities for everyone. Take a ride on the FireChaser Express roller coaster. This roller coaster sends you backward and forward!

Try out the bumper cars before heading to Dollywood's Splash Country. This water park inside Dollywood has waterslides, pools, and rivers to float on. If you're a thrill seeker, you'll want to try out the Butterfly. You'll drop down two slides that are 55 feet (17 meters) long. If you're looking to relax, grab a tube and enjoy the Downbound Float Trip. Take in the scenery of the Smoky Mountains as you float along.

Be sure to check out all the craft shops across Dollywood. You can visit the Woodcarving Shop and watch as special figurines are made. Or maybe you'd like to stop at the Sweet Shoppe for some candy. End your day at one of the many concerts the park hosts. If you're lucky, you may even get a chance to hear Dolly sing!

Dolly Parton is one of country music's most popular performers.

Watch as fresh homemade caramel is made at the Sweet Shoppe.

THE LOST SEA ADVENTURE

> If you're looking for an adventure belowground, head to the town of Sweetwater. You'll find the Lost Sea here. *The Guinness World Records* book lists it as the United States' largest underground lake. Scuba divers have explored the lake and still have not found where it ends.

Join a guided tour of the caverns. Check out the cool rock formations on the cave walls. Some of them are known as cave flowers. They are rare and found in only a few other caves in the world. After walking through the caves, climb aboard a glass-bottom boat. The second part of the tour takes you on a ride on the Lost Sea. You'll be surprised by how calm the lake is without wind.

Some special tours offer even more adventure. A guide will lead you into areas of the cave where few people have been. You can put on a hard hat and crawl through cracks and crevices. See the tracks of an ancient jaguar that died in the cavern twenty thousand years ago. You'll also see rooms where Civil War soldiers mined for saltpeter, an ingredient in gunpowder.

After your cave tour, check out Old Sweetwater Village. It is a replica of a village from the 1800s. It is a popular place to grab a snack.

On your boat tour, you'll explore the caves and see more of the underground lake rock formations.

TENNESSEE LANDFORMS

Tennessee is home to more caves than any other state in the nation. More than ninety-six hundred caves have been discovered so far! Bristol Caverns, Forbidden Caverns, and Raccoon Mountain Caverns are just a few.

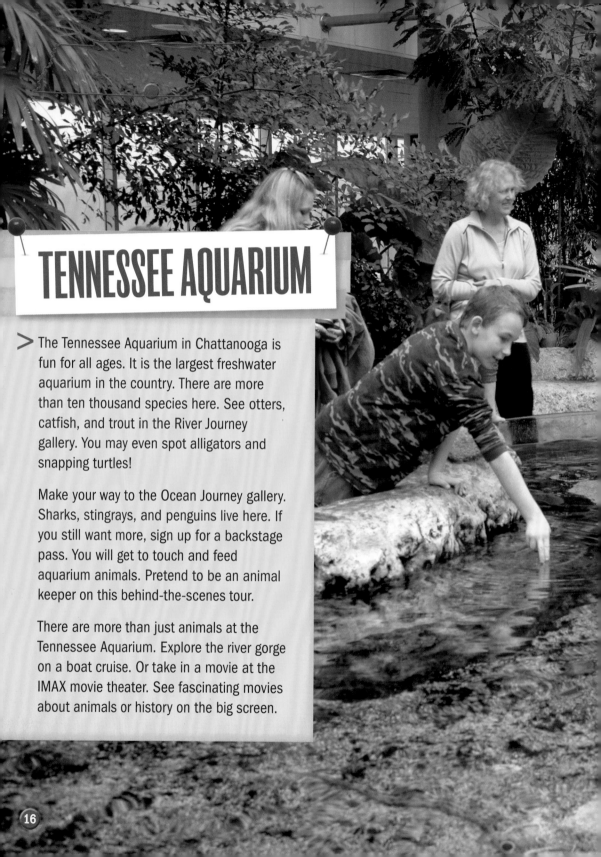

TENNESSEE AQUARIUM

> The Tennessee Aquarium in Chattanooga is fun for all ages. It is the largest freshwater aquarium in the country. There are more than ten thousand species here. See otters, catfish, and trout in the River Journey gallery. You may even spot alligators and snapping turtles!

Make your way to the Ocean Journey gallery. Sharks, stingrays, and penguins live here. If you still want more, sign up for a backstage pass. You will get to touch and feed aquarium animals. Pretend to be an animal keeper on this behind-the-scenes tour.

There are more than just animals at the Tennessee Aquarium. Explore the river gorge on a boat cruise. Or take in a movie at the IMAX movie theater. See fascinating movies about animals or history on the big screen.

Cruise down the river as an aquarium naturalist points out animals and historic areas.

End your day with a movie at the biggest theater in Chattanooga.

LOOKOUT MOUNTAIN

> There's a lot to see and do at Lookout Mountain in the Chattanooga area. Start the day at Ruby Falls. Here you'll see the nation's deepest cave and largest underground waterfall. Climb the Lookout Mountain Tower for great views of the Tennessee River. Visit the field nearby where the Battle of Missionary Ridge took place during the Civil War.

Next, make your way to Rock City Park. This nature park features enormous caves, oddly shaped boulders, and rock formations that are 200 million years old. Take a walk across the 200-foot (61 m) Swing-a-Long Bridge. It moves as you walk!

End the day riding the Incline Railway to the top of Lookout Mountain. Enjoy the scenery as you ride the world's steepest passenger railway. Visit the machine room to see the giant gears that move the railcars. From the top of the mountain, you'll see Chattanooga Valley.

The Ruby Falls waterfall is 145 feet (44 m) tall.

The Incline Railway has been running to the top of Lookout Mountain since 1895.

SHILOH NATIONAL MILITARY PARK

Walk through buildings at the park, including a replica of Shiloh Meeting House.

> Shiloh is one of the most well-preserved Civil War battle sites in the country. Shiloh National Military Park marks the site where one of the biggest battles of the Civil War (1861–1865) was fought. Visit the museum to see soldiers' uniforms, their weapons, and many other artifacts. Walk the land where the fighting took place. The park offers many demonstrations and reenactments. You can watch a realistic battle being fought.

Learn from costumed actors how to load and fire a cannon. There are more than two hundred Civil War cannons in the park. Listen to what daily life was like during the Civil War. Learn about the jobs different people had.

Stop at the visitor center or ask a park ranger for Civil War trading cards. Each card tells the story of a person or place involved in the Civil War.

End your visit with a car tour. This 13-mile (20 km) tour has twenty stops to enjoy. You'll see battlefields and homes used by military officials.

PICKING SIDES

During the Civil War, Tennessee joined the Confederacy. It was the last state to leave the Union. Many people living in Tennessee stayed true to the Union, however. After the war ended, Tennessee rejoined the Union. It is the only state with a monument honoring both the Union and Confederate armies. The monument is located on the lawn of the Greene County Courthouse in Greeneville.

MEMPHIS

> Memphis is known as the home of blues music. It has been the center of southern music since the 1900s. Attend the Beale Street Music Festival in May. You will hear popular musicians from around the world. Stop at nearby Graceland, the home of Elvis Presley. Tour his mansion and trophy building. Make sure to see the Elvis Presley Car Museum too.

Memphis is known for having its own unique style of barbecue. Try something new at one of Memphis's many restaurants. Maybe you would like deep-fried vegetables. Chicken and biscuits are another popular meal. Or attend the World Championship Barbecue Cooking Contest in May. Sign up to judge more than one hundred teams!

MEMPHIS BLUES

Blues music first became popular in the 1900s. W. C. Handy's "Memphis Blues" played in the music clubs. The blues is a unique style of music. It combines African American rhythms and melodies with European music traditions.

After touring the inside of Graceland, visit the Meditation Garden where Elvis Presley and some members of his family are laid to rest.

THE PEABODY DUCK MARCH

> If you're visiting Memphis, you won't want to miss the Peabody Duck March. This event has been happening daily at the Peabody Memphis hotel since the 1930s. Famous ducks live here in the Royal Duck Palace. Every morning at eleven o'clock, the Peabody Duckmaster arrives on the roof of the hotel. He leads the ducks to the elevator and down to the lobby. Join the crowds and watch as the ducks waddle across a special red carpet. They even have their own theme song! If you miss the morning march, you can see the ducks march back to their rooftop palace at five o'clock in the afternoon.

If you cannot see the ducks at the hotel, look for them on TV or in magazines. If you watched *Sesame Street* when you were younger, you may have seen the Peabody ducks. They helped Bert and Ernie celebrate Rubber Ducky Day.

YOUR TOP TEN!

Now that you have read about ten awesome things to see and do in Tennessee, think about what your Tennessee top ten list would include. What would you like to see if you visited the state? What would you like to do there? What would you be most excited for if you were planning a Tennessee vacation? These are all questions to consider as you ponder your own top tens. Write down your top ten list. If you'd like, you can even turn your list into a book and illustrate it with drawings or with pictures from the Internet or magazines.

The Peabody Duckmaster leads the ducks to and from their hotel rooftop home each day.

The ducks spend the afternoon swimming and splashing in the hotel lobby fountain.

TENNESSEE BY MAP

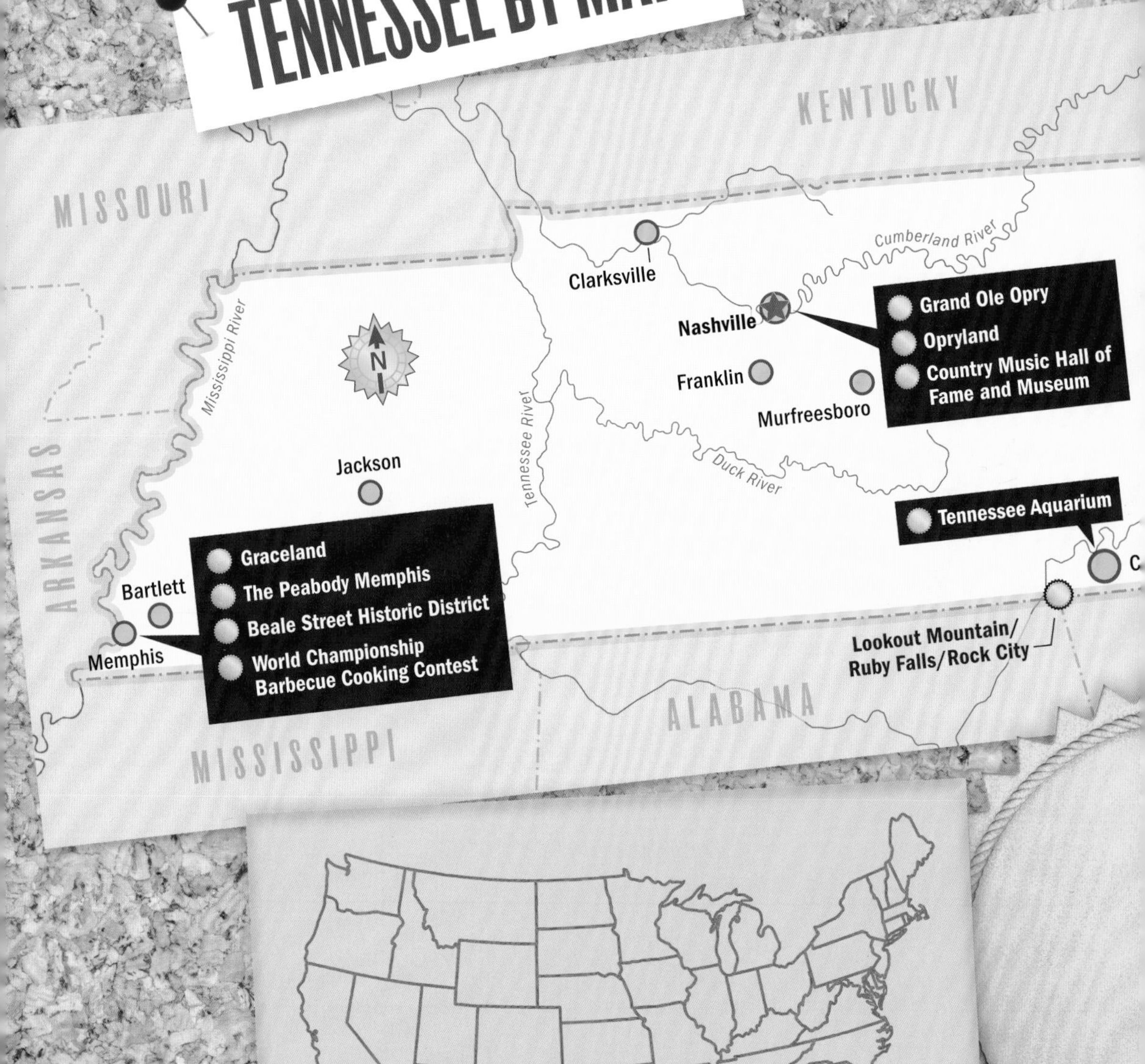

KENTUCKY

MISSOURI

Cumberland River

Clarksville

Nashville

Mississippi River

Grand Ole Opry

Opryland

Country Music Hall of Fame and Museum

N

Franklin

Murfreesboro

Duck River

Jackson

Tennessee River

ARKANSAS

Tennessee Aquarium

Graceland

The Peabody Memphis

Beale Street Historic District

World Championship Barbecue Cooking Contest

Bartlett

Memphis

Lookout Mountain/ Ruby Falls/Rock City

MISSISSIPPI

ALABAMA

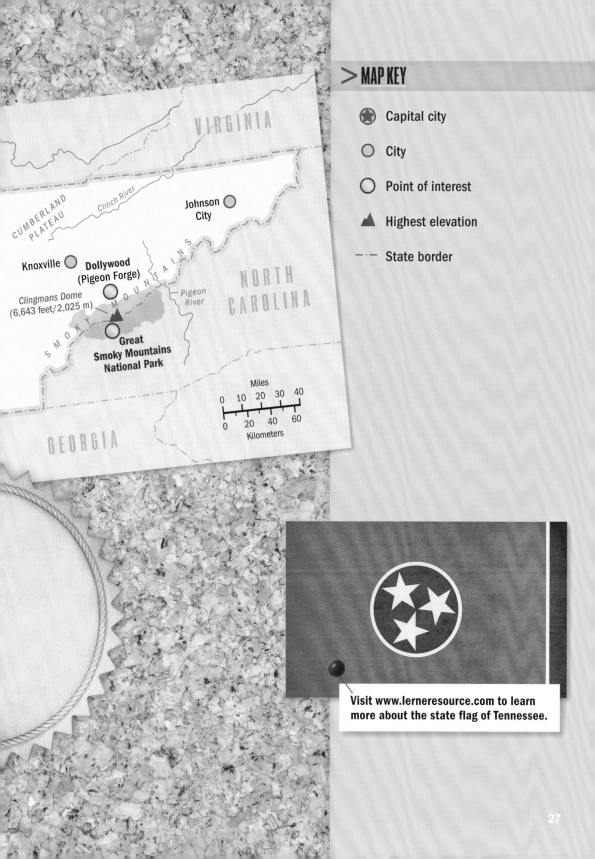

Capital city

City

Point of interest

Highest elevation

State border

VIRGINIA

CUMBERLAND PLATEAU

Clinch River

Johnson City

Knoxville

Dollywood (Pigeon Forge)

Clingmans Dome (6,643 feet/2,025 m)

S M O K Y   M O U N T A I N S

Pigeon River

NORTH CAROLINA

Great Smoky Mountains National Park

GEORGIA

Miles
0   10   20   30   40

0   20   40   60
Kilometers

Visit www.lernerresource.com to learn more about the state flag of Tennessee.

TENNESSEE FACTS

NICKNAME: The Volunteer State

SONG: "Tennessee" by Vivian Rorie, adopted in 1992

MOTTO: "Agriculture and Commerce"

FLOWERS: passionflower, iris

TREE: tulip poplar

BIRDS: mockingbird, bobwhite quail

ANIMALS: raccoon, box turtle, largemouth bass

FOODS: tomato, milk

DATE AND RANK OF STATEHOOD: June 1, 1796; the 16th state

CAPITAL: Nashville

AREA: 41,235 square miles (106,798 sq. km)

AVERAGE JANUARY TEMPERATURE: 37.5°F (3°C)

AVERAGE JULY TEMPERATURE: 79.5°F (26.3°C)

POPULATION AND RANK: 6,456,243, 17th (2012)

MAJOR CITIES AND POPULATIONS: Memphis (655,155), Nashville (624,496), Knoxville (182,200), Chattanooga (171,279), Clarksville (142,519)

NUMBER OF US CONGRESS MEMBERS: 9 representatives, 2 senators

NUMBER OF ELECTORAL VOTES: 11

NATURAL RESOURCES: limestone, coal, oil, natural gas, timber

AGRICULTURAL PRODUCTS: cattle, soybeans, chicken, corn, cotton, tomatoes, eggs, wheat, apples, peaches

MANUFACTURED GOODS: grain products, automobiles, boats, aircraft equipment

STATE HOLIDAYS OR CELEBRATIONS: Beale Street Music Festival, World Championship Barbecue Cooking Contest

GLOSSARY

artifact: a simple object that shows human work and represents a culture

banjo: a musical instrument with a round body like a drum, a long neck, and four or five strings

booth: a small enclosure giving privacy to one person

Confederacy: the Confederate States of America made up of the eleven southern states that withdrew from the United States in 1860 and 1861

demonstration: an action showing how an item is used

gorge: a narrow, steep-walled canyon

monument: a marker that identifies a place of historic interest or natural beauty

reenactment: a performance of something that has already happened

replica: an exact or close copy of something

rotunda: a large, round room

tradition: a belief or custom handed down through generations

Union: the northern US states that opposed the Confederacy

FURTHER INFORMATION

Semchuk, Rosann. *Tennessee: The Volunteer State*. New York: Weigl Publishers, 2012. This book offers a lot of information about Tennessee in a fun, travel-guide format.

Somervill, Barbara A. *Tennessee*. New York: Children's Press, 2014. This thorough guide explores Tennessee's history, culture, geography, and commerce.

Tennessee Facts
http://www.ipl.org/div/stateknow/tn1.html
This website offers many facts about the state of Tennessee, as well as kid-friendly links to help you learn even more.

Tennessee History for Kids
http://www.tnhistoryforkids.org/places
This cool website lets you visit some of the most interesting places in Tennessee with just a click of the mouse!

Tennessee Vacation—Tennessee for Kids
http://www.tnvacation.com/kids
Check out this website to find more places to visit on your Tennessee vacation.

LERNER

SOURCE

Expand learning beyond the printed book. Download free, complementary educational resources for this book from our website, www.lerneresource.com.

INDEX

Adams, 8

Adventure Science Center, 6

Beale Street Music Festival, 22

Bell Witch Cave, 8

Cades Cove Loop Road, 10

Chattanooga, 16, 18

Chattanooga Valley, 18

Cherokee American Indians, 10

Civil War, 14, 20

Clingmans Dome, 10

Country Music Hall of Fame and Museum, 6

Dollywood, 12

Graceland, 22

Grand Ole Opry, 6

Great Smoky Mountains National Park, 10

Greeneville, 20

Handy, W. C., 22

Lookout Mountain, 18

Lost Sea, 14

Memphis, 4, 22, 24

Nashville, 4, 6

Parton, Dolly, 12

Peabody Duck March, 24

Peabody Memphis, 24

Pigeon River, 10

Presley, Elvis, 22

Rock City Park, 18

Ruby Falls, 18

Shiloh National Military Park, 20

Smoky Mountains, 4, 10, 12

Sweetwater, 14

Tennessee Aquarium, 4, 16

Tennessee River, 4

Trail of Tears, 10

World Championship Barbecue Cooking Contest, 22

PHOTO ACKNOWLEDGMENTS

The images in this book are used with the permission of: © Dean Fikar/Thinkstock, p. 1; © benkrut/Thinkstock, p. 4; © Sean Pavone Photo/Thinkstock, p. 5 (bottom); © Laura Westlund/Independent Picture Service, pp. 5 (top), 26–27; © Mark Humphrey/AP Images, pp. 6–7, 8–9; © Sean Pavone Photo/iStockphoto, p. 7 (top), 7 (bottom); M.V. Ingram, p. 9 (left), 9 (right); © iStockphoto/Thinkstock, pp. 10–11; Public Domain, p. 10; Library of Congress, pp. 11 (HAER TENN, 78-GAT.V,6B--11), 20 (bottom) (LC-USZ62-67941); © Oliver Gerhard/Glow Images, pp. 12–13, 13 (bottom); © Helga Esteb/Shutterstock Images, p. 13 (top); © gracious_tiger/Shutterstock Images, pp. 14–15, 15 (bottom); © Clayton Sharrard/Thinkstock, p. 15 (top); © James Schwabel/Alamy, pp. 16–17; © Tennessee Aquarium/MCT/Newscom, p. 17 (top); © Rob Hainer/Shutterstock Images, p. 17 (bottom); © Melinda Fawver/Shutterstock Images, pp. 18–19; © IrinaK/Shutterstock Images, p. 19 (top); © Jon Spaull/DK Images, p. 19 (bottom); Shiloh National Military Park, pp. 20–21; © Brian Swartz/Thinkstock, p. 20 (top); © Natalia Bratslavsky/Shutterstock Images, pp. 22–23; Theron C. Bennett Publishing/Library of Congress, p. 22; © Simplyphotos/Thinkstock, p. 23; © The Peabody Memphis/AP Images, pp. 24–25; © Richard Gardner/Rex USA, p. 25 (left), 25 (right); © nicoolay/iStockphoto, p. 27; © Richard Gunion/Thinkstock, p. 29 (top right); © Robert Blanchard/Thinkstock, p. 29 (middle left); © Deyan Georgiev/Thinkstock, p. 29 (bottom right); © Mark Stout/Thinkstock, p. 29 (bottom left).